Why Should You Eat Healthful Foods?

by Mrs. Deckard's class
with Tony Stead

capstone
classroom

We think eating healthful food
is very important.

One reason is because it helps
you be strong.

Another reason is because it helps you to not be sick.

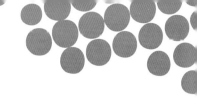

A final reason is because it helps you live a long life.

Eating healthful food is important if you want to stay fit and strong.

8

Yummy! Healthful foods
are great!

Healthful foods are good for you because they have vitamins.

Vitamin c
makes you
Stronger !

Eating healthful foods helps you grow and be smart.

13

Did you know that eating eggs is good for you because they are a protein and make you smarter?

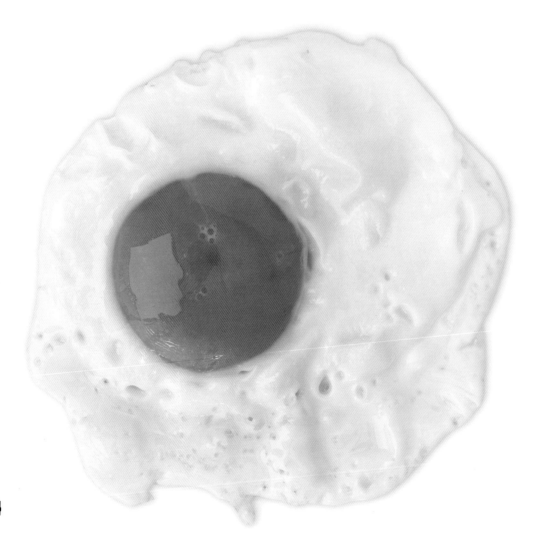

There are many foods from which to choose.

What choices can you make to eat more healthfully?